PATRI

MAHOMES

BIOGRAPHY

CLIFF SOWLE

Disclaimer:

This is a work of nonfiction. All efforts have been made to provide accurate information, but some events or conversations may be reconstructed based on available sources and the author's research. Any errors or omissions are unintentional.

Table of contents

Chapter 1 - Roots and Rise

Texas Roots

Patrick Mahomes' story begins in Tyler, Texas, a town steeped in the traditions of Friday night lights and a deep love for football. Born on September 17, 1995, to Pat Mahomes Sr. and Randi Martin, young Patrick was immersed in a world of sports from the very beginning.

His father, Pat Mahomes Sr., was a Major League Baseball pitcher, introducing Patrick to the competitive spirit and dedication required in professional sports. While baseball was a significant presence in his early years, with Patrick even serving as a batboy for his dad's teams, it was the gridiron that ultimately captured his heart.

Growing up in Whitehouse, Texas, Patrick attended Whitehouse High School, where his athletic talents blossomed. He excelled not only in football but also in baseball and basketball, showcasing his natural athleticism and competitive drive. This multi-sport background played a crucial role in developing his exceptional hand-eye coordination, agility, and ability to read the field – skills that would later translate into his unique quarterbacking style.

Beyond his father's athletic career, Patrick's family provided a strong foundation of support and instilled values that shaped his character. His mother, Randi, was a constant source of encouragement, emphasizing the importance of education and hard work alongside his athletic pursuits.

His godfather, LaTroy Hawkins, another former MLB pitcher, also served as a mentor, offering guidance and sharing his experiences in professional sports. This network of strong male role models instilled in Patrick a sense of discipline, resilience, and the importance of giving back to the community.

While football eventually became his primary focus, Patrick's early involvement in baseball and basketball significantly contributed to his overall athletic development. Baseball honed his throwing mechanics and accuracy, while basketball fostered his court awareness, agility, and ability to improvise.

These diverse athletic experiences helped him develop a unique skillset that set him apart on the football field. His ability to throw from different arm angles, his incredible no-look passes, and his knack for escaping pressure and extending plays are all testament to the benefits of his multi-sport background.

Even in his youth, there were glimpses of the extraordinary talent that would make Patrick Mahomes a household name. He possessed a natural arm talent, throwing a football with exceptional velocity and accuracy from a young age.

His coaches and teammates recognized his leadership qualities and his ability to elevate the play of those around him. It was clear that Patrick had a special gift, and his dedication to honing his skills set the stage for his future success.

This exploration of Patrick Mahomes' Texas roots provides a glimpse into the formative experiences and influences that shaped the young athlete. From his family's athletic background to his multi-sport journey, these early chapters laid the foundation for the legendary quarterback he would become.

Gridiron Calling

While Patrick Mahomes displayed athletic prowess across various sports in his youth, his destiny ultimately lay on the football field. At Whitehouse High School, he transitioned from a versatile athlete to a rising gridiron star, captivating audiences with his exceptional talent and leadership.

Initially, Mahomes dabbled in various positions, showcasing his versatility as a safety and even a linebacker. However, it was his arm talent and playmaking ability that truly shone through, eventually leading him to the quarterback position. This decision proved to be a turning point, not only for Mahomes but for the future of football itself.

Mahomes' high school career was nothing short of spectacular. As the quarterback for the Whitehouse Wildcats, he led his team to remarkable victories, shattering records along the way. His ability to throw the ball with incredible power and precision, coupled with his improvisational skills and elusiveness, made him a force to be reckoned with.

He threw for over 4,600 yards and 50 touchdowns in his senior year alone, earning him numerous accolades, including the East Texas Player of the Year award. His performances on the field drew attention from college scouts across the country, solidifying his status as one of the nation's top high school quarterback prospects.

While Mahomes enjoyed success in baseball and basketball, his passion for football and his natural talent as a quarterback ultimately led him to focus on the gridiron. This decision wasn't merely about choosing a sport; it was about embracing a calling.

He recognized that his unique skillset and leadership qualities were best suited for the quarterback position.

The ability to orchestrate an offense, make split-second decisions under pressure, and inspire his teammates resonated deeply with him.

Moreover, Mahomes saw the potential to redefine the quarterback position with his unconventional playing style. His ability to throw from different arm angles, complete no-look passes, and extend plays outside the pocket hinted at a new era of quarterbacking, one that prioritized creativity and improvisation.

Mahomes' decision to focus on quarterback not only shaped his own destiny but also had a profound impact on the landscape of football. His electrifying playing style and remarkable success have inspired a new generation of quarterbacks, encouraging them to embrace their creativity and push the boundaries of what's possible on the field.

His high school years served as a proving ground, where he honed his skills and developed the confidence to pursue his dreams. The "Gridiron Calling" was clear, and Mahomes answered with unwavering determination, setting the stage for a legendary career that would redefine the quarterback position and captivate fans worldwide.

Red Raider Days

Patrick Mahomes' journey to NFL stardom took a pivotal turn during his college years at Texas Tech University. Choosing to stay in his home state, he donned the iconic red and black uniform of the Red Raiders, where he would further hone his skills and solidify his reputation as an exceptional quarterback with a truly unique playing style.

His time in Lubbock wasn't just about racking up impressive statistics; it was a period of intense growth and development, where he embraced the freedom and creativity that would become hallmarks of his game.

At Texas Tech, Mahomes thrived under the tutelage of head coach Kliff Kingsbury, a proponent of the "Air Raid" offense. This offensive scheme, known for its emphasis on passing and spreading the field, provided the perfect environment for Mahomes to flourish.

He was given the freedom to make reads at the line of scrimmage, change plays, and utilize his arm strength to attack defenses downfield. This experience allowed him to develop his ability to read defenses, make quick decisions, and deliver accurate throws under pressure.

While the Air Raid offense provided a framework, Mahomes' natural talent and improvisational skills truly set him apart. He became known for his unorthodox throws, including sidearm passes, no-look passes, and throws on the run, often leaving spectators and opponents in awe.

This unconventional style was a product of both his natural athleticism and his willingness to take risks. He wasn't afraid to break the mold of a traditional pocket passer, relying on his instincts and creativity to make plays that seemed impossible.

Mahomes' time at Texas Tech was marked by a series of record-breaking performances. He amassed an incredible 11,252 passing yards and 93 touchdowns in just three seasons, showcasing his remarkable productivity and efficiency.

In 2016, his final year at Texas Tech, he led the nation in passing yards (5,052), passing touchdowns (41), and total offense (5,319 yards). These achievements solidified his status as one of the most exciting and dynamic quarterbacks in college football.

Beyond the impressive numbers, Mahomes' time at Texas Tech was crucial for his development as a leader and a competitor. He learned to command the huddle, rally his teammates, and persevere through adversity.

He also gained valuable experience playing against top competition in the Big 12 conference, facing off against future NFL players and honing his skills against some of the best defenses in the country.

Mahomes' college years at Texas Tech were a transformative period in his journey. He embraced the freedom of the Air Raid offense, honed his unique playing style, and established himself as one of the nation's top quarterbacks.

His time as a Red Raider provided the foundation for his future success in the NFL, where he would continue to dazzle fans and rewrite the rules of quarterbacking.

Draft Day Destiny

The 2017 NFL Draft marked a pivotal moment in Patrick Mahomes' life, a turning point that would launch him into the national spotlight and set the stage for his meteoric rise in the NFL. After a stellar college career at Texas Tech, Mahomes's name was buzzing among scouts and analysts, but questions lingered about his transition to the professional level.

However, the Kansas City Chiefs, led by head coach Andy Reid and general manager John Dorsey, saw something special in the young quarterback. They recognized his raw talent, his exceptional arm strength, and his potential to become a game-changer in the NFL.

Leading up to the draft, Mahomes participated in the NFL Combine, where he showcased his athleticism and impressed scouts with his arm talent. He also held private workouts for several teams, including the Chiefs, further solidifying his position as a top quarterback prospect.

Despite the hype, there were concerns about his "gunslinger" mentality and his experience in the Air Raid offense. Some analysts questioned whether his improvisational style would translate to the NFL, where defenses are faster and more complex.

The Chiefs, holding the 27th overall pick, were determined to secure Mahomes. Recognizing that other teams were also interested in the talented quarterback, they made a bold move, trading up with the Buffalo Bills to acquire the 10th overall pick.

This trade involved sending their 27th pick, a third-round pick, and a future first-round pick to the Bills, a significant investment that demonstrated their belief in Mahomes's potential.

On April 27, 2017, the moment arrived. With the 10th overall pick, the Kansas City Chiefs selected Patrick Mahomes, officially welcoming him into the NFL. The announcement was met with excitement and anticipation, as Chiefs fans eagerly awaited the arrival of their new quarterback.

For Mahomes, it was a dream come true. He had reached the pinnacle of professional football, joining a storied franchise with a rich history. The opportunity to learn from Andy Reid, a renowned quarterback guru, and play alongside established stars like Travis Kelce and Tyreek Hill, was a perfect scenario for his development.

The Chiefs' decision to draft Mahomes was not without risk. They already had a veteran quarterback in Alex Smith, who had led the team to consistent success. However, they recognized that Mahomes possessed a rare talent that could elevate the franchise to new heights.

This calculated risk paid off handsomely. Mahomes spent his rookie season learning from Smith, absorbing the complexities of the NFL game and preparing for his opportunity to shine.

The 2017 NFL Draft marked the beginning of a new era for the Kansas City Chiefs. The selection of Patrick Mahomes would transform the franchise, ushering in a period of unprecedented success and excitement.

His arrival brought a sense of optimism and anticipation to Kansas City. Fans eagerly awaited the moment when Mahomes would take the reins and unleash his electrifying playing style on the NFL. Little did they know that they were witnessing the dawn of a new era in quarterbacking, one that would redefine the possibilities on the football field.

Chapter 2 - Chiefs Kingdom

Learning the Ropes

Patrick Mahomes' arrival in Kansas City marked the beginning of an exciting new chapter, but it wasn't an immediate jump to superstardom. The Chiefs had a plan in place, one that emphasized patient development and learning from a seasoned veteran. This strategy proved crucial in shaping Mahomes into the elite quarterback he is today. His early years in the NFL were defined by absorbing knowledge, honing his skills, and building a strong foundation under the guidance of Alex Smith.

Mahomes' rookie season in 2017 was primarily spent observing and learning. The Chiefs, led by the experienced Alex Smith, were playoff contenders, and there was no need to rush the young quarterback into action. This provided Mahomes with a valuable opportunity to acclimate to the NFL without the immediate pressure of leading the team.

He diligently attended meetings, studied film, and practiced alongside Smith, absorbing the nuances of the professional game. This period allowed him to understand the complexities of NFL offenses, defenses, and game strategies at a deeper level.

The relationship between Mahomes and Smith was crucial during this period. Smith, a respected veteran with a reputation for his professionalism and leadership, served as an ideal mentor for the young quarterback.

He provided guidance on and off the field, sharing his knowledge of the game, offering advice on preparation and decision-making, and demonstrating the importance of leadership and work ethic.

Smith's influence extended beyond the technical aspects of the game. He instilled in Mahomes the importance of professionalism, humility, and dedication, qualities that would serve him well throughout his career.

While Mahomes' rookie season was primarily focused on learning, he did get a taste of NFL action. In Week 17, with the Chiefs having already secured their playoff spot, Mahomes made his first career start against the Denver Broncos.

This game provided a glimpse of his potential, as he showcased his arm talent and playmaking ability, throwing for 284 yards and completing 22 of 35 passes. While the Chiefs lost a close game, Mahomes' performance generated excitement and anticipation for the future.

Mahomes' early years in the NFL were a period of preparation and growth. He embraced the opportunity to learn from a veteran quarterback, absorbing knowledge and developing his skills under the guidance of a respected mentor.

This patient approach allowed him to build a strong foundation for his future success. He entered the league with immense talent, but his time learning the ropes under Alex Smith proved invaluable in shaping him into the complete quarterback who would soon take the NFL by storm.

The Chiefs' decision to allow Mahomes to learn and develop before thrusting him into the spotlight was a testament to their long-term vision. They recognized his potential and provided him with the ideal environment to flourish. This strategy would pay dividends in the years to come, as Mahomes emerged as one of the most electrifying and dominant quarterbacks in NFL history.

The Breakout Season

After a year of patient observation and learning under Alex Smith, Patrick Mahomes' moment arrived. The 2018 season marked his official takeover as the Kansas City Chiefs' starting quarterback, and he wasted no time in making a resounding statement. What followed was a season for the ages, a mesmerizing display of talent, skill, and athleticism that captivated the NFL and launched Mahomes into superstardom.

With Alex Smith traded to the Washington Redskins, the keys to the Chiefs' offense were handed to Mahomes. The anticipation was palpable, with fans and analysts eager to see what the young quarterback could do with a full season at the helm.

Mahomes exceeded all expectations. From the very first game, he unleashed his unique brand of football, a captivating blend of arm strength, accuracy, and improvisational brilliance that left defenses bewildered.

Mahomes' 2018 season was a statistical marvel. He threw for a staggering 5,097 yards and 50 touchdowns, joining Peyton Manning as the only quarterbacks in NFL history to reach both milestones in a single season.

He led the league in touchdown passes and finished second in passing yards, showcasing his remarkable efficiency and productivity. His ability to connect with receivers downfield, make throws from different arm angles, and extend plays outside the pocket made him a nightmare for opposing defenses.

Beyond the impressive numbers, Mahomes' 2018 season was filled with jaw-dropping plays that showcased his exceptional talent and creativity. His "no-look" passes became a signature move, leaving defenders guessing and fans in awe.

He threw touchdowns from seemingly impossible angles, escaped pressure with Houdini-like elusiveness, and consistently delivered in clutch moments. His ability to make something out of nothing, turning broken plays into spectacular gains, became a defining characteristic of his game.

Mahomes' individual brilliance translated into team success. He led the Chiefs to a 12-4 record and the top seed in the AFC playoffs. The team's offense, fueled by Mahomes' arm and playmaking ability, became one of the most explosive and entertaining units in the league.

The Chiefs' home stadium, Arrowhead Stadium, became a cauldron of excitement, with fans chanting "MVP!" as Mahomes orchestrated the team's high-powered attack.

Mahomes' remarkable performance earned him the NFL's Most Valuable Player award, a testament to his impact on the league and his team's success. At just 23 years old, he became one of the youngest players to receive this prestigious honor.

His MVP season solidified his status as a rising star in the NFL, a quarterback with the potential to redefine the position and lead the Chiefs to a new era of dominance.

Patrick Mahomes' 2018 season was a breakout campaign that exceeded all expectations. He exploded onto the scene as a starter, captivating the

NFL with his exceptional talent, creativity, and leadership.

His performance not only earned him individual accolades but also propelled the Chiefs to the top of the AFC. This season marked the beginning of Mahomes' reign as one of the league's most electrifying and dominant quarterbacks, a player whose impact would be felt for years to come.

Super Bowl Glory

The 2019-2020 NFL season was a thrilling ride for the Kansas City Chiefs, culminating in a triumphant Super Bowl victory that etched their names in NFL history. At the heart of this success was Patrick Mahomes, the young quarterback who had already established himself as a force to be reckoned with. Super Bowl LIV, against the formidable San Francisco 49ers, would be his ultimate test, a chance to cement his legacy and bring the Lombardi Trophy back to Kansas City after a 50-year drought.

The Chiefs entered the playoffs as a powerhouse, fueled by Mahomes' exceptional playmaking and an explosive offense. They navigated through the AFC playoffs with determination, overcoming deficits and showcasing their resilience.

In the AFC Championship game against the Tennessee Titans, they found themselves trailing by 10 points, but Mahomes orchestrated a remarkable comeback, leading the Chiefs to a 35-24 victory and securing their place in Super Bowl LIV.

The Super Bowl matchup against the San Francisco 49ers presented a formidable challenge. The 49ers boasted a dominant defense and a powerful running game, posing a significant threat to the Chiefs' high-flying offense.

The game was a tense affair, with both teams trading blows. The 49ers took a 20-10 lead in the fourth quarter, and the Chiefs found themselves facing adversity.

With the championship on the line, Mahomes rose to the occasion. He orchestrated a series of scoring drives, displaying his exceptional arm talent, poise under pressure, and ability to make clutch plays.

He connected with Tyreek Hill for a crucial 44-yard gain, setting up a touchdown pass to Travis Kelce. He then led another scoring drive, capped off by a 5-yard touchdown pass to Damien Williams, giving the Chiefs a 24-20 lead.

The Chiefs' defense, led by Chris Jones and Tyrann Mathieu, stepped up in the final minutes, forcing a turnover on downs and securing the victory. Damien Williams added another touchdown with a 38-yard run, sealing the Chiefs' 31-20 triumph.

Mahomes' performance in the fourth quarter was nothing short of legendary. He completed 8 of 13 passes for 114 yards and two touchdowns, showcasing his ability to deliver when it mattered most.

Mahomes was named the Super Bowl MVP, a fitting recognition of his exceptional performance and leadership. He became the second-youngest quarterback to win the award, further solidifying his place among the NFL's elite.

Super Bowl LIV was a defining moment for Patrick Mahomes and the Kansas City Chiefs. It was a testament to their resilience, their teamwork, and their unwavering belief in their young quarterback.

The victory brought an end to a 50-year championship drought, fulfilling a lifelong dream for Chiefs fans and cementing Mahomes' legacy as a Super Bowl champion.

Mahomes' performance in Super Bowl LIV will be remembered as one of the greatest in Super Bowl history. He showcased his exceptional talent, leadership, and clutch playmaking ability, leading the Chiefs to a historic victory.

This Super Bowl triumph marked a significant milestone in Mahomes' career, solidifying his status as a generational talent and a champion. It was a moment of glory that will forever be etched in the annals of NFL history.

Overcoming Adversity

Patrick Mahomes' journey to NFL stardom hasn't been without its share of obstacles. Like any athlete, he's faced injuries, setbacks, and moments of doubt. But what truly sets Mahomes apart is his unwavering resilience, his ability to bounce back from adversity and emerge even stronger. He's proven time and again that he's not just a talented quarterback, but a true competitor with an indomitable spirit.

Mahomes has faced several significant injuries throughout his career, testing his physical and mental fortitude. In 2019, he suffered a dislocated kneecap that threatened to derail his season. However, he displayed remarkable determination, returning to action ahead of schedule and leading the Chiefs to a Super Bowl victory.

In 2021, he played through a turf toe injury during the playoffs, showcasing his toughness and commitment to his team. And most recently, in the 2023 playoffs, he battled a high ankle sprain, yet still delivered a gutsy performance to help the Chiefs reach the Super Bowl.

These injuries have tested Mahomes' physical limits, but they've also revealed his mental strength and his unwavering dedication to the game. He's consistently demonstrated a remarkable ability to overcome pain and adversity, inspiring his teammates and fans alike.

Beyond injuries, Mahomes has faced numerous challenges on the field. Opposing defenses have devised strategies to contain his explosive playmaking, forcing him to adapt and evolve his game.

He's faced double teams, blitz packages, and complex coverages designed to limit his options. Yet, Mahomes has consistently found ways to overcome these challenges, showcasing his intelligence, adaptability, and ability to read defenses.

He's learned to adjust his game plan, utilize his check-down options, and make quick decisions under pressure. These experiences have honed his skills and made him an even more complete quarterback.

Not every game or season has been a triumph for Mahomes. He's experienced losses, setbacks, and moments of self-doubt. But even in the face of adversity, he's maintained a positive attitude and a relentless work ethic.

He's used setbacks as opportunities for growth, analyzing his mistakes, learning from his experiences, and coming back stronger. This ability to learn and adapt is a testament to his maturity and his commitment to continuous improvement.

Mahomes' ability to overcome adversity is a testament to his character and his unwavering determination. He's proven that he's not just a talented athlete, but a true competitor who thrives in the face of challenges.

His resilience has inspired his teammates, his fans, and aspiring athletes around the world. He's shown that with hard work, dedication, and a positive mindset, it's possible to overcome any obstacle and achieve greatness.

Patrick Mahomes' journey is a powerful reminder that adversity is an inevitable part of life, but it doesn't have to define us. His ability to overcome injuries, challenges, and setbacks is an inspiration to all.

He's shown that with resilience, determination, and a positive attitude, we can emerge from difficult times stronger and more determined than ever. Mahomes' story is a testament to the human spirit's ability to triumph over adversity and achieve extraordinary things.

A Dynasty in the Making

Patrick Mahomes and the Kansas City Chiefs aren't just a flash in the pan; they're building a dynasty. Since his breakout season in 2018, the team has been a consistent force in the NFL, reaching remarkable heights and solidifying their claim as one of the most dominant teams of this era. With Mahomes at the helm, they've achieved a level of sustained success that puts them in the conversation with some of the greatest dynasties in NFL history.

The Chiefs have been a perennial playoff team since Mahomes took over as the starting quarterback. They've won their division title an impressive six consecutive times, showcasing their dominance in the AFC West. This consistent regular season success has provided a strong foundation for their deep playoff runs.

Mahomes has already led the Chiefs to three Super Bowl appearances in his young career, a remarkable feat that speaks volumes about his leadership and the team's overall strength. They won Super Bowl LIV against the San Francisco 49ers and Super Bowl LVII against the Philadelphia Eagles, cementing their place among the NFL's elite.

Reaching the Super Bowl is a challenging endeavor, requiring a combination of talent, strategy, and a bit of luck. The fact that the Chiefs have achieved this multiple times in a short span highlights their exceptional quality and their commitment to excellence.

The Chiefs have hosted the AFC Championship game for an incredible five consecutive seasons, an unprecedented achievement in NFL history. This demonstrates their consistent dominance in the AFC and their ability to overcome tough competition in the playoffs.

Arrowhead Stadium has become a fortress during the playoffs, with the Chiefs feeding off the energy of their passionate fans. This home-field advantage has been a crucial factor in their success.

Beyond individual talent, the Chiefs have cultivated a winning culture that permeates the entire organization. From the coaching staff to the players, there's a shared commitment to excellence, hard work, and teamwork.

Head coach Andy Reid has instilled a disciplined and focused approach, while Mahomes' leadership and infectious enthusiasm have created a positive and driven atmosphere. This winning culture has been instrumental in the Chiefs' sustained success.

The NFL is a dynamic league, with teams constantly evolving and adapting their strategies. The Chiefs have shown a remarkable ability to adjust to these changes, maintaining their dominance despite facing new challenges each season.

Mahomes has continued to develop his game, adding new dimensions to his skillset and becoming an even more complete quarterback. The team has also made strategic roster moves, ensuring they have the right pieces in place to compete at the highest level.

The Kansas City Chiefs are building a dynasty that will be remembered for years to come. With Mahomes leading the way, they've achieved a level of sustained success that's rare in the NFL.

Their multiple Super Bowl appearances, AFC Championship game dominance, and consistent playoff contention have solidified their place among the league's elite. They've created a winning culture that fosters excellence and a legacy that will inspire future generations of players and fans.

The Chiefs' dynasty is still in the making, but their achievements thus far have been nothing short of remarkable. With Mahomes at the helm, the future looks bright for Kansas City, and their pursuit of greatness continues.

Chapter 3 - Beyond the Game

The Mahomes Magic

Patrick Mahomes is more than just a quarterback; he's a magician on the gridiron. His playing style is a captivating blend of athleticism, creativity, and exceptional skill, redefining what's possible at the quarterback position. He's a master of improvisation, capable of conjuring extraordinary plays out of seemingly impossible situations. Let's delve into the elements that make Mahomes so unique:

The foundation of Mahomes' magic is his incredible arm talent. He possesses exceptional arm strength, capable of launching the ball downfield with pinpoint accuracy. Whether it's a deep bomb or a threading the needle through tight coverage, Mahomes can deliver the ball with velocity and precision.

But his arm talent goes beyond just power. He can throw from various arm angles, sidearm, overhand, and even off-platform, making it incredibly difficult for defenders to anticipate his throws. This versatility keeps defenses guessing and opens up passing lanes that wouldn't be available to a conventional quarterback.

One of Mahomes' signature moves is the "no-look" pass, a deceptive technique that has become synonymous with his playing style. He'll look one way, drawing the defense's attention, then whip the ball in another direction to a wide-open receiver.

This audacious move requires exceptional awareness, timing, and trust in his receivers. It's a testament to his ability to manipulate defenses and create opportunities out of thin air. The no-look pass is not just a flashy trick; it's a calculated tactic that adds another layer of unpredictability to his game.

Mahomes thrives in chaos. When a play breaks down, he doesn't panic; he improvises. He'll escape the pocket, extend plays with his legs, and find receivers downfield with uncanny accuracy.

His ability to create something out of nothing is what truly sets him apart. He can turn a potential sack into a highlight-reel touchdown, leaving defenders grasping at air and fans in awe. This improvisational genius is a product of his athleticism, his vision, and his innate ability to process information quickly under pressure.

Mahomes' playing style is characterized by creativity and unpredictability. He's not afraid to break the mold of a traditional quarterback, constantly pushing the boundaries of what's possible on the field.

He'll throw passes from seemingly impossible angles, complete throws on the run, and make plays that defy logic. This unorthodox approach keeps defenses off balance and makes him a constant threat to score from anywhere on the field.

Mahomes is a master of deception. He uses his eyes, his body language, and his pre-snap movements to manipulate defenders and create opportunities for his offense.

He'll look off receivers, pump fake, and use his mobility to keep defenses guessing. This ability to deceive and misdirect is crucial to his success, allowing him to create separation for his receivers and exploit weaknesses in the defense.

Mahomes' playing style has had a profound impact on the NFL. He's inspired a new generation of quarterbacks, encouraging them to embrace their creativity and push the boundaries of the position.

His influence can be seen in the way young quarterbacks are playing the game, with more emphasis on improvisation, mobility, and off-platform throws. Mahomes has redefined what it means to be a quarterback in the modern NFL, and his "magic" continues to captivate fans and revolutionize the game.

A Leader On and Off the Field

Patrick Mahomes is more than just a supremely talented quarterback; he's the heart and soul of the Kansas City Chiefs. His impact extends far beyond his on-field heroics, shaping the team's culture and inspiring those around him with his exceptional leadership qualities.

Mahomes is a leader by example. His relentless work ethic, dedication to his craft, and unwavering commitment to the team set a high standard for everyone in the organization. He's the first one in the building and the last one to leave, always striving to improve and push his teammates to be their best.

He doesn't shy away from challenges, consistently demonstrating a willingness to put in the extra effort and make sacrifices for the betterment of the team. This dedication inspires his teammates to follow suit, creating a culture of accountability and excellence.

Mahomes exudes a positive and infectious energy that permeates the entire Chiefs organization. His enthusiasm for the game is contagious, motivating his teammates and creating a fun and supportive environment.

He's always encouraging his teammates, celebrating their successes, and picking them up after setbacks. This positive attitude fosters a sense of camaraderie and unity, essential ingredients for a winning team.

Mahomes possesses an unwavering confidence that inspires confidence in those around him. He believes in his abilities and his team's potential, even in the face of adversity. This confidence translates into composure under pressure, allowing him to make smart decisions and lead his team to victory in clutch moments.

His teammates feed off this confidence, trusting his leadership and believing in their ability to overcome any challenge. This unwavering belief in themselves and their quarterback is a crucial factor in the Chiefs' success.

Mahomes is a selfless leader who empowers his teammates to shine. He recognizes their strengths and puts them in positions to succeed. He trusts his receivers to make plays, giving them the freedom to showcase their talents and contribute to the team's success.

This empowering leadership style fosters a sense of ownership and responsibility among his teammates. They feel valued and trusted, which motivates them to perform at their best and contribute to the team's collective goals.

Mahomes is a unifying force in the Chiefs' locker room. He brings players together, fostering a sense of camaraderie and shared purpose. He treats everyone with respect, regardless of their role on the team, creating an inclusive and supportive environment.

This ability to unite players from diverse backgrounds and with different personalities is a testament to his leadership skills. He creates a sense of belonging and shared purpose, essential for a team to thrive.

Mahomes' leadership extends beyond the football field. He's actively involved in the Kansas City community, using his platform to make a positive impact. He's involved in various charitable initiatives, supporting causes such as education, youth development, and social justice.

His commitment to giving back inspires others to follow his lead, creating a ripple effect of positive change in the community. He's a role model for young people, demonstrating the importance of using one's influence for good.

Patrick Mahomes is not just building a legacy of on-field greatness; he's also establishing himself as a leader of exceptional character and influence. His impact on the Kansas City Chiefs extends far beyond his remarkable playing abilities.

He's a leader by example, inspiring his teammates with his work ethic, dedication, and positive attitude. He empowers those around him, fosters a winning culture, and uses his platform to make a positive impact in the community.

Mahomes' leadership qualities are an integral part of the Chiefs' success, shaping the team's identity and driving their pursuit of greatness. He's a true leader on and off the field, leaving a lasting legacy that will inspire future generations of athletes and leaders.

Brand Mahomes

Patrick Mahomes isn't just a football superstar; he's a burgeoning business mogul. His on-field success has translated into a powerful personal brand, attracting lucrative endorsements, fueling smart business ventures, and solidifying his legacy beyond the gridiron. Mahomes understands the power of his platform and is strategically building an empire that extends far beyond his playing days.

Mahomes' marketability is undeniable. His charisma, talent, and positive image make him a highly sought-after endorser. He's partnered with a diverse range of brands, including:

- **Adidas:** Mahomes has a signature shoe line with Adidas, reflecting his style and influence in the world of sports fashion.

- **Oakley:** As the first NFL player to sign with Oakley, he's the face of their Prizm Optics line, showcasing sunglasses that blend performance and style.

- **State Farm:** Mahomes' appearances in State Farm commercials have become iconic, showcasing his humor and relatability.

- **Head & Shoulders:** He's become synonymous with the shampoo brand, promoting healthy hair and confidence.

- **Subway:** Mahomes has joined the Subway team, endorsing their healthier menu options and commitment to fresh ingredients.

- **Other notable partnerships:** He's also partnered with brands like Essentia Water, Hy-Vee, T-Mobile, and Molson Coors, demonstrating his wide appeal and diverse interests.

These endorsements not only generate significant income but also reinforce Mahomes' image as a successful and trustworthy figure. He carefully selects brands that align with his values and resonate with his fanbase.

Savvy Business Ventures:

Mahomes isn't just collecting endorsement checks; he's actively investing in his future. He's involved in various business ventures, including:

- **Sports Ownership:** He's a part-owner of several professional sports teams,

including the Kansas City
Royals (MLB), Sporting Kansas
City (MLS), the Kansas City
Current (NWSL), and even the
Alpine F1 team. These
investments demonstrate his
passion for sports and his
business acumen.

- **15 and the Mahomies
  Foundation:** His foundation
  focuses on improving the lives
  of children through initiatives
  that support health, wellness,
  and education. This
  philanthropic endeavor
  showcases his commitment to
  giving back to the community.

- **Whoop:** He's an investor in
  Whoop, a wearable technology
  company that provides fitness
  and health tracking data. This
  investment aligns with his

interest in technology and performance optimization.

- **Prime Hydration:** Mahomes has partnered with Logan Paul to launch Prime Hydration, a sports drink company that has quickly become a competitor to established brands like Gatorade. This venture highlights his entrepreneurial spirit and his ability to identify market opportunities.

Mahomes is strategically building a legacy that extends far beyond his playing career. He's leveraging his success on the field to create a lasting impact in the business world and the community.

His endorsements, business ventures, and philanthropic efforts are all part of a larger plan to build a brand that stands for excellence, innovation, and social responsibility. He's creating a platform that will allow him to continue making a difference long after his football days are over.

Mahomes' entrepreneurial spirit and business savvy serve as an inspiration to young athletes and aspiring entrepreneurs. He's demonstrating that it's possible to achieve success both on and off the field, using one's platform to create opportunities and build a lasting legacy.

His story is a testament to the power of hard work, dedication, and strategic thinking. He's proving that athletes can be more than just entertainers; they can be successful business leaders and agents of positive change.

Patrick Mahomes is more than just a football player; he's a brand. His name is synonymous with success, innovation, and leadership. He's built a powerful platform through endorsements, business ventures, and philanthropy, solidifying his legacy as a true icon both on and off the field.

His journey is an inspiration to all, demonstrating the power of leveraging one's talents and influence to create a lasting impact. Brand Mahomes is a force to be reckoned with, and its influence will continue to grow for years to come.

Family Man

While Patrick Mahomes thrives in the spotlight as a football superstar, he also cherishes his role as a devoted family man. His relationship with his wife, Brittany Matthews, and their growing family provides a grounding force in his life, offering a sense of normalcy and balance amidst the whirlwind of his NFL career.

Patrick and Brittany's love story is one that has captured the hearts of many. Their relationship dates back to their high school days in Whitehouse, Texas, where they first met as young athletes with shared dreams and aspirations. Their bond grew stronger over the years, evolving from teenage sweethearts to life partners.

Their love story has unfolded in the public eye, with fans witnessing their journey from prom dates to engaged couple to proud parents. Their enduring relationship is a testament to their commitment, support, and shared values.

Patrick and Brittany's family has blossomed in recent years. They welcomed their first child, Sterling Skye Mahomes, in February 2021. The arrival of their daughter brought immense joy and a new dimension to their lives.

Mahomes embraces his role as a father with enthusiasm and dedication. He cherishes the moments spent with his daughter, sharing glimpses of their family life on social media and expressing his love and pride for his growing family.

In November 2022, they expanded their family with the arrival of their son, Patrick "Bronze" Lavon Mahomes III. The addition of a son further enriched their family dynamic, creating a loving and supportive environment for their children to thrive.

Balancing the demands of an NFL career with the responsibilities of fatherhood is no easy feat, but Mahomes navigates this challenge with grace and determination. He prioritizes his family, making time for them amidst his busy schedule.

He's often seen bringing his daughter to practices and games, creating heartwarming moments that showcase his dedication to both his family and his team. He's a role model for other athletes, demonstrating that it's possible to excel in their careers while also being present and involved fathers.

Brittany Matthews is more than just Patrick's wife; she's his biggest supporter and a constant source of strength. She's a former professional soccer player and a successful fitness entrepreneur, balancing her own career aspirations with her role as a mother and wife.

Brittany is a constant presence at Patrick's games, cheering him on from the sidelines and celebrating his successes. She's also a vocal advocate for her husband, defending him against criticism and celebrating his achievements.

Their partnership is built on mutual respect, support, and shared dreams. They navigate the challenges of their busy lives together, providing a strong foundation for their family.

Patrick Mahomes often emphasizes the importance of family in his life. He credits his parents and his wife for their unwavering support, acknowledging their role in his success both on and off the field.

He values the sense of normalcy and stability that his family provides, offering a refuge from the pressures of his high-profile career. His family is his anchor, providing him with the love, support, and balance he needs to thrive.

Patrick Mahomes is a role model for family values. He demonstrates that it's possible to achieve greatness in one's career while also prioritizing family and cherishing the joys of fatherhood.

His dedication to his wife and children, his commitment to balancing his personal and professional life, and his public displays of affection for his family inspire others to prioritize their own family relationships.

Patrick Mahomes' journey is not just about individual achievement; it's a family affair. His wife, children, and extended family are an integral part of his story, providing him with the love, support, and motivation to excel in all aspects of his life.

He embraces his role as a family man with pride and dedication, demonstrating that family is the foundation upon which his success is built. The Mahomes family is a testament to the power of love, commitment, and shared values, inspiring others to cherish their own family bonds and build a legacy of love and support.

Giving Back

Patrick Mahomes is a firm believer in using his platform for good. He understands the influence he holds and actively engages in charitable work and community involvement, inspiring the next generation to make a positive impact. His efforts extend beyond simply writing a check; he's actively involved in initiatives that support youth development, health, and social justice.

15 and the Mahomies Foundation:

At the heart of Mahomes' philanthropic endeavors is his foundation, 15 and the Mahomies. Established in 2019, the foundation focuses on improving the lives of children in need. It supports initiatives that promote health, wellness, education, and overall well-being.

The foundation's programs include:

- **15 for 15:** This program provides grants to 15 youth organizations annually, supporting their efforts to make a difference in their communities.

- **Mahomes Magic Crunch:** Partnering with PLB Sports & Entertainment, Mahomes launched a cereal brand with a portion of the proceeds benefiting his foundation.

- **Community events:** The foundation hosts various events throughout the year, including youth football camps, fundraising galas, and community outreach programs.

Mahomes has a strong connection with Children's Mercy Hospital in Kansas City. He's made significant donations to the hospital, supporting their efforts to provide world-class healthcare to children in need.

He's also visited the hospital numerous times, spending time with patients, offering encouragement, and brightening their day. His presence brings joy to the children and their families, demonstrating his compassion and commitment to making a difference.

Mahomes has been vocal about social justice issues, using his platform to advocate for equality and raise awareness about systemic injustices. He was one of the prominent voices in the NFL's "Inspire Change" campaign, promoting social justice and racial equality.

He's also used his social media presence to speak out against racial injustice and encourage his followers to get involved in creating a more equitable society. His willingness to use his platform to address these important issues demonstrates his leadership and commitment to positive change.

Mahomes' dedication to giving back serves as an inspiration to young people. He demonstrates that success isn't just about personal achievements; it's also about making a positive impact on the world.

He encourages young athletes to use their platform for good, emphasizing the importance of giving back to their communities and inspiring others to follow their lead. His actions speak louder than words, setting an example for the next generation to follow.

Mahomes is a role model for community involvement. He demonstrates that even amidst a demanding NFL career, it's possible to make time for charitable work and give back to those in need.

His efforts inspire others to get involved in their communities, whether it's through volunteering, donating, or simply spreading awareness about important causes. He's creating a ripple effect of positive change, encouraging others to join him in making a difference.

Patrick Mahomes is building a legacy that extends far beyond the football field. His charitable work, community involvement, and social justice advocacy demonstrate his commitment to making a positive impact on the world.

He's inspiring the next generation to use their platform for good, creating a legacy of giving back that will have a lasting impact on countless lives. His actions embody the true spirit of sportsmanship and leadership, demonstrating that success is not just about individual achievements but also about making a difference in the lives of others.

Chapter 4 - The Future of Mahomes

Chasing Records

Patrick Mahomes is already considered one of the greatest quarterbacks in NFL history, and he's only just begun. At 28 years old, he's achieved a level of success that most players only dream of. But Mahomes isn't satisfied with past accomplishments; he's driven to etch his name at the very top of the NFL record books. With his exceptional talent, relentless work ethic, and a supportive team around him, he has the potential to shatter numerous records and solidify his place as a legend.

Mahomes' early career achievements are nothing short of remarkable. He's already won two Super Bowl MVP awards, two NFL MVP awards, and led the Chiefs to five consecutive AFC Championship games. He holds the record for the most passing yards in a player's first 100 games and is on pace to become the fastest quarterback to reach 30,000 career passing yards.

This early dominance sets the stage for a historic career. He's already surpassed many legendary quarterbacks in terms of early career achievements, and he's only getting started.

Mahomes has the potential to break numerous NFL records, including:

- **Career Passing Yards:** The current record is held by Tom Brady with 89,214 yards. Given Mahomes' exceptional passing ability and his relatively young age, he has a legitimate chance to surpass this mark.

- **Career Passing Touchdowns:** Brady also holds this record with 649 touchdowns. Mahomes is already well on his way, and with his knack for finding the end zone, he could very well break this record too.

- **Most Super Bowl Wins:** Tom Brady holds the record with 7 Super Bowl wins. Mahomes has already won two, and with the Chiefs' continued success, he could challenge this seemingly insurmountable record.

- **Most MVP Awards:** Peyton Manning holds the record with 5 MVP awards. Mahomes has already won two, and if he continues his dominant play, he could surpass Manning's mark.

Several factors contribute to Mahomes' potential to break these records:

- **Exceptional Talent:** Mahomes possesses a rare combination of arm talent, athleticism, and football IQ that sets him apart from his peers.

- **Offensive System:** The Chiefs' offensive system, designed by Andy Reid, is perfectly suited to Mahomes' strengths, allowing him to maximize his potential.

- **Elite Supporting Cast:** Mahomes is surrounded by a talented supporting cast, including Travis Kelce, one of the greatest tight ends in NFL history.

- **Durability:** While he's faced some injuries, Mahomes has generally been durable throughout his career, which is crucial for longevity and record-breaking potential.

- **Longevity:** If Mahomes can maintain his current level of play and avoid major injuries, he could play well into his late 30s or even early 40s, giving him ample time to chase these records.

Mahomes' pursuit of NFL records is not just about personal glory; it's about cementing his legacy as one of the greatest quarterbacks of all time. He's driven to leave an indelible mark on the game, inspiring future generations of players and fans.

His impact on the NFL is already undeniable. He's redefined the quarterback position with his unique playing style and exceptional talent. He's led the Chiefs to unprecedented success, creating a dynasty that will be remembered for years to come.

Mahomes' chase for records is a testament to his ambition, his dedication, and his unwavering pursuit of greatness. He's not just playing for the present; he's playing for a place in history. And with his talent, determination, and the support of his team, he has the potential to achieve legendary status.

The Evolution of a Quarterback

Patrick Mahomes is a generational talent, blessed with a unique set of physical gifts and an almost preternatural understanding of the game. But what truly sets him apart is his capacity for growth and adaptation. He understands that the NFL is a constantly evolving landscape, and to maintain his elite status, he must continually refine his game. This commitment to evolution, coupled with his dedication to physical and mental well-being, sets the stage for a long and prosperous career in the league.

In his early years, Mahomes was known for his "gunslinger" mentality, a fearless approach that prioritized big plays and improvisation. He wowed audiences with his no-look passes, sidearm throws, and uncanny ability to escape pressure and extend plays. This style was undeniably effective, leading to record-breaking performances and early championship success.

However, as defenses adapted and the league became more familiar with his tendencies, Mahomes recognized the need to evolve. He began to prioritize efficiency over highlight-reel plays, focusing on making smart decisions and taking what the defense gave him. He refined his pre-snap reads, improved his pocket presence, and became more adept at utilizing his check-down options.

This evolution showcased his maturity as a quarterback. He understood that longevity in the NFL requires more than just raw talent; it demands adaptability, intelligence, and a willingness to refine one's game.

Mahomes has often described playing quarterback as a "chess match," a strategic battle of wits against opposing defenses. He's become increasingly adept at dissecting defenses, recognizing coverages, and anticipating pressure schemes.

This strategic approach has allowed him to become a more complete quarterback. He's not just reacting to what he sees; he's anticipating and manipulating defenses, dictating the flow of the game with his mind as much as his arm.

Mahomes understands that longevity in the NFL requires more than just skill; it demands physical and mental resilience. He's committed to maintaining peak physical condition through rigorous training, nutrition, and recovery protocols.

He also prioritizes his mental health, recognizing the importance of managing stress, staying focused, and maintaining a positive mindset. This holistic approach to well-being sets the stage for a long and career.

The NFL is a league of constant change, with rosters evolving from year to year. Mahomes has demonstrated his ability to adapt to these changes, maintaining his elite level of play despite shifts in personnel.

He's built strong chemistry with new receivers, adjusted to different offensive line configurations, and continued to thrive despite facing new challenges each season. This adaptability is a testament to his leadership, his football IQ, and his ability to elevate the play of those around him.

Mahomes' journey of evolution is far from over. He's constantly seeking new ways to improve, studying film, working with coaches, and pushing himself to become the best version of himself.

As the league continues to evolve, Mahomes will undoubtedly adapt, adding new dimensions to his game and finding innovative ways to maintain his edge. His commitment to growth and his unwavering pursuit of excellence ensure that he will remain a force to be reckoned with for years to come.

Patrick Mahomes' evolution as a quarterback is a testament to his dedication, his intelligence, and his unwavering commitment to excellence. He's a model for longevity in the NFL, demonstrating that adaptability, continuous improvement, and a holistic approach to well-being are crucial for sustained success.

His journey inspires young quarterbacks and veterans alike, proving that greatness is not a destination but a continuous pursuit. Mahomes' commitment to evolution ensures that he will remain a dominant force in the NFL, captivating audiences and leaving a lasting legacy on the game.

Mahomes' Legacy

Patrick Mahomes is more than just a quarterback; he's a cultural icon who is redefining the way the game is played and inspiring a new generation of athletes. His impact on football extends far beyond his impressive statistics and championship trophies. He's a trailblazer who is changing the perception of the quarterback position, encouraging creativity, and promoting a positive image for the sport.

Mahomes has ushered in a new era of quarterback play, one that prioritizes improvisation, athleticism, and playmaking ability. He's shattered the mold of the traditional pocket passer, demonstrating that quarterbacks can be dynamic athletes who create magic outside the pocket.

His "no-look" passes, sidearm throws, and ability to extend plays have become signature moves, inspiring young quarterbacks to embrace their creativity and push the boundaries of what's possible. He's shown that quarterbacks can be more than just game managers; they can be game-changers.

Mahomes' playing style is a testament to the power of creativity and innovation. He's not afraid to take risks, try new things, and challenge conventional wisdom. This approach has not only led to spectacular plays on the field but has also inspired a new wave of quarterbacks who are willing to think outside the box.

Young athletes are now encouraged to embrace their individuality, experiment with different techniques, and find new ways to express themselves on the field. Mahomes has shown that football can be a canvas for creativity, where imagination and innovation are celebrated.

Mahomes is a role model both on and off the field. He's known for his sportsmanship, his humility, and his dedication to his community. He's a positive ambassador for the sport, inspiring young people with his work ethic, his leadership, and his commitment to excellence.

In an era where athletes are often scrutinized for their behavior, Mahomes stands out as a beacon of positivity. He represents the best of what sports can be, demonstrating that athletic achievement can go hand-in-hand with character and integrity.

Mahomes' influence on youth football is undeniable. Young players are emulating his playing style, practicing his signature moves, and adopting his fearless mentality. He's become a hero to aspiring quarterbacks, inspiring them to dream big and work hard to achieve their goals.

His impact extends beyond just quarterbacks. Young athletes across all positions are inspired by his dedication, his passion, and his unwavering belief in himself. He's shown them that with hard work, determination, and a positive attitude, anything is possible.

Mahomes' legacy will extend far beyond his playing days. He's not just a football player; he's a cultural icon who has changed the way the game is played and inspired a generation of athletes.

His impact on football will be felt for years to come, as young players continue to emulate his style, embrace his creativity, and strive to achieve the level of greatness he has attained. He's leaving a lasting legacy that will shape the future of the sport and inspire countless young people to pursue their dreams.

Patrick Mahomes is more than just an athlete; he's an inspiration. He's shown the world that with talent, dedication, and a positive attitude, you can achieve extraordinary things. He's revolutionized the quarterback position, inspired creativity and innovation, and promoted a positive image for the sport.

His legacy will be one of greatness, both on and off the field. He's a role model for young athletes, demonstrating that success is not just about individual achievements but also about making a positive impact on the world. Mahomes' impact on football and his influence on the next generation of athletes will be felt for generations to come.

Milton Keynes UK
Ingram Content Group UK Ltd.
UKHW022138291124
451915UK00011B/754